Arc

Arc

David Clarke

Nine
Arches
Press

Arc
David Clarke

ISBN: 978-0-9931201-5-2

Cover artwork © Eleanor Bennett
www.eleanorleonnebennett.com

First published September 2015 by:

Nine Arches Press
PO Box 6269
Rugby
CV21 9NL
United Kingdom

www.ninearchespress.com

Printed in Britain by:
The Russell Press Ltd.

This book is for Malcolm

Contents

Throw   11

Epic Fail
The Messengers   15
Lyre   16
Dear Superman,   17
Epic Fail   18
Votive   19
Philosophy of Cake   20
Queer   21
Why I Moved to London   22
Scott Walker Sonnet   23
At Kirkgate Market   24
A Harmony for Spring   25
A Provincial Recital   26

Permanent Emergency
Sword-Swallowing for Beginners   29
The Psychiatrist Addresses His Patient, a Soldier   30
Asklepieion of Epidauros   31
Permanent Emergency   32
Reading Habits   33
Lenin at the Music Hall   34
Elaborate Moustache   35
Notes Towards a Definition of the Revolution   36
Patrick J Hinds   38
October 1962   40
You Explain to Me Your Plans for Surviving the   42
     End of Civilization as We Know It
How It Was   43
A Journey   44

Arcadia

Song of His Sooterkin Brother 47
Murder Ballad 48
To the Harvesters of Ambergris 49
The End of a Film with Jimmy Stewart 50
Driving Back to Lincolnshire for a Funeral 51
Paysage marin 53
Ode to Achilles 54
In Hangzhou 55
Exodus 56
Substance 58

    Candy
    1/8
    Gran Reserva
    Halfzware Shag
    Powder

Boats 61

From Here

A Family Romance 65
From Here 67
On Assembling and Disassembling
   a Greenhouse 68
See England by Train 70
News from Home 71
To *The Gloucestershire Echo* 72
Domestic Gods 73
Shed 74
than you expected 75
For Hanna on Her 50th Birthday 76
About the Ocean 77
House of the Artist 78
Author Photograph 79

Notes & Acknowledgements 81

Throw

I am the boy who threw the ball
         into summer's empty mouth
then saw there was no void at all –

as at the zenith of my lob
         the sun's hot lozenge stuck like tar
and held my missile's arc aloft

for seconds, minutes, hours it seemed.
         Dark jewel set in a golden ring,
black pupil stitched with molten seam,

agate globe in quartz's kiss,
         iron plunged in an ember pit –
little eclipse and apocalypse.

I squinted to see where it would land,
running forward with empty hands.

Epic Fail

The Messengers

Hark!, the angels are crying. We do not hear.
Even while they pace the lime-washed halls
brandishing bold lilies, as if to direct
our spiritual traffic – we are nonplussed.

We turn the pages of magazines, inspect
the sorry heel of our own dangled shoe.
Hark! and *Hark!* again. The rain is dashing
redbrick walls, cars illuminate

the prosey night, while ministers of all
religions bob home to a book or spouse –
and every one just out of earshot
for seraphim, *Hark!*-ing themselves hoarse.

Not even poets attend to that hailing,
haloed in their screen-bright fug.
Such barren shores they choose to call to,
those heralds. Such blasted shores.

Lyre

Orpheus wants two Americanos.
His mate is impatient on double yellows
in the van where they keep the harp,
rapping the roof with his knuckles.
Our godly axeman flashes a victory V,
thus drives home the point

     of the goth girl's pen
     tracing cutely bulbous capitals
     on her yellow pad, endlessly redrafting
     a PERSONAL STATEMENT
     as she chews on a hank of purple hair

          that curtains the puffy eyes
          of the barista. He slouches,
          hung-over, to the steam machine
          with a face full of shrapnel,
          stomach turning at that burnt
          milk smell of hot babies

     screaming in 4x4s. Half-bald pigeons,
     cyclists in eye-watering Lycra,
     the whole ragged street tensed
     beyond the café windows

waiting for Orpheus to swing
back into his van and strike
the morning's opening chord.

Dear Superman,

I know, sometimes we have to take our chances.
But even now I feel like every shiver
in the air could be you passing. Asses
still need whipping and you're such a giver –
giving them hell, I mean. Those freaks who slither
in every gutter spell plenty of printer's ink.
Pictures of you turning a swollen river,
zapping the chains of captives, link by link.
Such meek-seeming schoolboy manners. You flush so pink

at the world's praise. Looking back, I cringe to think
how I'd lie awake to watch for a chink
of light beneath our bedroom door, the mirror
showing a failed sidekick, tired of the stink
of battle on your cape. Not thinking bigger
than the two of us, I'd never linger
on news of disaster. You'd scoot to salvage NASA's
latest screw-up. I'd long to see you dither,
shyly reach for your alter ego's glasses.

Epic Fail

The pelicans in St James' Park are preening
on their artificial rock, presenting
pieces of themselves for inspection –
their wings like clattering plates of armour.

They rattle sabre bills against their chests,
sprinkle white and grey confetti of feathers
onto the island's setting of luminous algae.
This could be the point to introduce

the peculiar legend of how they feed their young
on their own blood – which is another way
of saying there is a rage in beauty
and, indeed, a beauty in rage.

But theirs is not the only display.
A young man swaggers across the park with his lover,
fizzing with much loud and nervous talk,
while another arrives in sportswear, to bounce from foot

to foot like huffing a gazelle, and others strut
in suits with slightly loosened ties and an air
of fevered purpose. I'd like, you understand,
to somehow bring this back to the pelicans,

folded on their haunches now in a stupor.
Such creatures, though, don't really care who looks
at them or how, unlike the occasional tourists
who trot to the shin-high railing that circles the lake,

their cameras held at arm's length. We capture
ourselves in the moment, such as we can.

Votive

From the Lithuanian

A tough crew. The quay is lit with voices
of trucks – their axles buck like the talk of poets, their sacrilege.
Allow them this great panorama, the tough crew
who dunk their candles in holy water,
a rude maze spun among the painted hulls and sails.
José, anachronistically chivalrous, plucks his small banjo.

The true buccaneers are the poets, he sings, they jog the lights
of heaven and make them weep, however oddly such men
    are slain.
The quay now matted with candles, looking-glasses,
maps of the cape, instruments for bending zephyrs, fauns.
Now the maze grows ever more a maze. It keeps its scent,
rank as any satyr's.

Philosophy of Cake

So, Plato reckoned all cake
the image of cake's idea –
the ur-cake, cake's essence, was echoed
in every humble sponge, each fancy

eased from greasy parchment,
and in all those ramparts of mid-
European kirsch and cream,
the balls of choux spritzed fat

with crème patissière. And so
I slice and bite again and again
in hope of tasting what cake is
in truth, the sweetness of that truth,

its give and clag between the teeth,
but find my hunger still unstilled,
my ideal portion yet unserved.

Queer

At first with his thumbnail and spit,
       then with the edge of a coin, the teeth
of a key, he scrapes at each unseriffed
       stroke of luscious magic marker,
marring each letter of that sneering
       monosyllable, its languorous
freight of vowels. But not at the circle
       that circumscribes his name in black,
or at the parallel bars of the equals sign
       that pin him to the fearful
five-letter word – an icon made
       of two same things that lie
so close, making more than themselves
       of themselves. The cisterns' echoing,
monkish in the cavernous afternoon,
       plinks among distant playground sounds.
Wafts of disinfectant and playing fields.

Why I Moved to London

When they named me bigot of the year
for the second time, I knew I had to leave that town.
No more skulking in the discount bookshop,
waiting for someone to buy my misery memoir.
It was either that or finish as one of those sods
who uses the factory pre-set ring-tone, unable to choose
between hauteur and clownish self-deprecation.
Flood memory was the latest buzz-word for social scientists,
but the road to the railway station stretched beyond infinity.
The following decade went something like this –
I struggled for forms of artistic practice to engage
an already-jaded public. I walked each morning
from Chalk Farm into Bloomsbury. With certain
kinds of weather, the streets allowed a sense of liberation.

Scott Walker Sonnet

Crossed-legged on the floor in your manager's office,
you brushed at chords to show the arranger
that rain should sound like sorrow unreleased.
Strings quivered at the pitch of sad pleasure.

Suddenly, fans outgrew you – no strangers dreamt
of your hands, your smile. Years of cover versions.
Easy listening spiralled down to a run-out
groove that ticked the time away.

You lift the arm, pull a cap low over
your eyes, hunch through wind-churned streets
to a studio booth – Muffled in echo-less air
that raises hairs on your skin.

So, begin again
with only your voice and the dark.

At Kirkgate Market

They hang like candles in their shimmer of fat,
or bouts of huge, unvarnished violins.
De-wheeled motorbikes, they are stripped of their cogs,
the pistons of their rumination seized.

They smell like a box of fisherman's maggots,
tumbling in a fist of sawdust heat,
or, on the pantry slab, that pot of grease
gone milky as an old dog's eye.

Blades slice decisions into their shapes,
slit the pink upholsteries of flesh
and bind them anew into fibrous books,
the bones sliced through like sections of planets.

In halls of chill white tile and mirror
meat pools between trims of plastic grass.
Beneath the glass, lush mounds of tongue and liver
are gleaming in the way of a private treasure.

A Harmony for Spring

When sun makes lakelets of suburban window panes
and March has struggled into its itchy suit of spring,
when love performs its unapplauded legerdemain –

I tie the burlap sack of myself in a cunning knot,
sample the air with its hint of herbs and hen-warm eggs,
tap at asphalt with tireless feet and wake strange thoughts

in the mind of that giant whose skull we populate like fleas.
Dumb old world. Red steam rising off
black fields shakes out a blue that's ripe for bristled bees,

and flowerheads, like dessicated rubber bands,
distend and give, then roll out lolling amber tongues.
My strolling pace will metronome this saraband

of sap and dust, experimental birdsong trims
the lanes, and in the softest burrows, dreys and lairs
birth unfurls those cries which are its synonyms.

A Provincial Recital

The boys of the ballet sweat in the small theatre.
Blinded by a curtain of stage-light, they smile
and gesture into darkness, infer us like
the audience of gods, which, in our way,

we are – Sour gods with bags of wine gums,
ponderous in head and limb, who crumple
programmes in old fists as the boys strain
to lift their rigid doll-girls, those diagrams

of birds. From the stalls, we watch each muscle
shift and perspiration bead pale panes
of skin. Squeeze-box ribs deflate, breath breaks
in shallow waves across their stomachs. And then

they kick the ground from under their feet,
flowing out, above, beyond the dance.

Permanent Emergency

Sword-Swallowing for Beginners

Start by flicking the fleshy switch at the back
of your throat. When you've thrown up a dozen times,
you'll find the impulse subsides – you can sit for hours
with a knuckle softly pressed inside your head,

watching rolling news of the war. Insert spoons,
knitting needles, a length of plumber's pipe.
Stare at the ceiling, your jaw loose as a gorging
python's, and try to conjure those shocks that pass

through the body, but leave it intact – the rasp of panicked
breath, the whump of a nearby explosion, a scream.
Or think of the soldier who coughed up a sleeping bullet,
shrapnel burrowing out of a human thigh

to freedom. By then you'll be ready to take a blunted
bayonet, silver and slick with spit. Arrange
your body around that deathly spindle,
repeat to yourself – I am unharmed. Unharmed.

The Psychiatrist Addresses His Patient, a Soldier

*'In France, Clovis Vincent quickly became known for his
"persuasive" methods. [...] Vincent was a devotee of the
use of high-strength galvanic current, which he combined
with injunctions to get well, or even with threats when
the patient refused to recover.'*
  – Didier Fassin and Richard Rechtman

I ask my assistants to leave the room for you,
my special case, let the apparatus
lilt in its leather holster. Battle lines
are drawn so close, citizens fancy hearing

thumps of materiel that punch the land,
or swear they saw a flock of sooty sparrows
swirl with smoking tails. But here the harder
war is carefully waged. In white-washed rooms

men's bodies twist beneath my trembling hands,
crying for release from cowardice –
young skin pale as curds, through which the current
flows, the yelp of minds that find relief.

Resister – this struggle will not pass me by.
I too am martyred on this rubber bed,
a charge will also arc across my marrow
when I turn these dials. Just say the word.

Asklepieion of Epidauros

The priests insist I write the word *dream* in my poem,
claim it's a door for the healer. I pay them to kill
a kid-goat, but can't believe the dead will hear
the shriek of knives in Hades. Gore on marble,

guts in a brazier. They give me a part in their play –
I enter stage left, a stranger masked in distress
as the genre dictates. Another pilgrim plunges
his blade, spilling a fist-full of scarlet ribbon.

Air swells hot with pine and hotter granite
as they carry me to the temple of sleep. A maze
turns in on itself like a dozing snake.
If the god will enter my mind he'll find it broken.

Permanent Emergency

We find ourselves on a marbled concourse,
    the air tart, the thievery elegant.

We find ourselves flailing in cataracts of red dust,
    our ears ringing at the pitch of the aftershock.

We find ourselves quarantined in the media compound,
    living off shrink-wrapped carbs.

We find ourselves nodding to the security detail,
    the exact nature of their remit.

We find ourselves lobbying for *hearts and minds*,
    drumming our fingers on the conference table's
        mahogany veneer.

We find ourselves offering flexible consultancy options,
    straightening our zany neck-ties.

We find ourselves schmoozing the policy-wonks,
    a post-traumatic pastoral.

Reading Habits

Do you still have my copy of *Ultimate Hard Bastards*?
I remember we'd spend evenings perusing the mugs
of broken-featured men, those tattooed thugs
papped on courthouse steps. No shaken-not-stirreds

in white tuxedos there – motors of hate
revved in their skulls as they stalked greasy side-streets,
marking their manor's borders in body heat.
We imagined shiv and shooter would not equivocate,

that they'd speak desires no one could misconstrue –
but those handy geezers, now raddled and fixed in black
and white, have lost their rage and kept their lack.
They know, like us, that only the lack is true.

Lenin at the Music Hall

The tight-rope artiste levels her spangled body,
airy antithesis to the stubborn thesis of gravity.
Vladimir sees the grace of the dialectic
spun in her ribboned limbs. The boozy comic,
who apes an aristocrat down on his luck, knows more
of the struggle, its ironies, than all those long-bearded bores
in Siberian taverns. His twist of monkey-nuts grows damp
in his hand as the conjurer's tassled assistant vamps
for the crowd, is sawn in half. A chain of silk handkerchiefs
is pulled from her mouth. A metaphor, Volodya perceives,
for the proletarian's lot – dazzled and dazed
by the very machine that enslaves him. The curtain is raised
for the final act, a soppy songbird's balladry.
He dabs his eyes. Such sentiment is reactionary.

Elaborate Moustache

It turned out to be my last mission.
Those goons cracked me like a cheap safe,

dumped me as a heap of clothes at the embassy gate.
Now I lurch in and out of night

as my people attempt to de-brief me.
They flood my veins with truth serum,

but all I get are flashes of that lonely bridge,
the mist waltzing to Central European time

as the dead wire buzzes in my ear
so loud I don't even notice my backup's cries.

The river swallows him whole, smacks
its grey lips. The cinnamon in that last coffee

was disguising something. A barman
grinned beneath his elaborate moustache,

turned damp glass against cloth with fighter's
hands, knuckles hatched with scars.

Notes Towards a Definition of the Revolution

The Revolution was a Young Pioneer,
photographed arm in arm with a round-cheeked
Polish peasant at a festival of world
youth; or it was a peacenik at a stall
of hectographed pamphlets and imported Soviet
imprints of Gorky's *The Mother*, harassed
by police in an arcade of the International
Style. Often it was an earnest

panel of intellectuals consuming
meat-paste sandwiches in a Sheffield Labour
Club in the mid 1970s; then again,
a summer camp for children of Belgian steelworkers,
who learned bright songs and fashioned likenesses
of Iosif Vissarionovich Dzhugashvili
in coloured drinking straws. In any case,
it was a committee meeting where all concurred,

a workers' palace picked out in sugary
pediments of Soviet Baroque, a whirligig
model of neutrons or satellites in perpetual
motion; yet, equally, the wife of a tireless trade
unionist, making her husband his supper
as he came home gone midnight from a march in the city.
Sometimes the Revolution was a stray
whose Stakhanovite master wired her to gizmos,

then watched through a telescope as she burned on re-entry.
But even then the Revolution
was still a walk in the People's Park—
it smelled of fresh paint and linoleum, sounded
like a folk song performed for a delegation.
The Revolution was, finally, a crudely
executed copy of Lenin's death-mask
on the walnut desk where the minister would slump,
insensible with revolutionary optimism.

Patrick J Hinds

d. 1 November 1914

My mother found the family name, spelled with *i*
    as our side does, cut in marble high up
    on the Menin Gate. She lit a candle,
    like the faithful of your shore-side church, their dead

about them in that world of ghosts and holy-holy,
    winters hard with rain. Even then their god
    was bowing out, his final gambits lost to slicing
    steel through earth and flesh. But if you thought

about these things, and guessed your place within it all,
    I couldn't know, although I've seen the lough, the ferry
    churning to and fro across the tide, across
    the troubled years. Your own sweet life of vital sense

and farm-boy strength was nothing but a moment's snag
    in that slow rhythm, a needle catching in its groove.
    When I was there at Castle Ward they showed us halls
    of mirrors, blind where mercury had slipped in time,

reminded us of mirror-makers barmy for the sake
    of that old trick of seeing ourselves. The lough's grey waters
    shifted, shivered, refused me sight of my own image,
    even the part that was my grandfather's, the brother who got

your names. You didn't live to see him born. He left
    that place to try his luck in England – too short-sighted,
    it turned out, to get himself shot, the Irish Guards
    left lighter by one man, who never wore a uniform

as you did in that photo, the only one I've seen,
    your country face grin-grimacing beneath a private's cap.
    If there were letters I bet they'd not have much to say,
    except the food and missing home. Then – vaporised

or flung to bits – your self would not have left much to
    return. But Patrick, your name nags at me, chiselled
    black and blank as time, unsounded still as we
    invent new pomps for lads like you in khaki

to perform, gone all teary on their sacrifice
    and yours, that never was, perhaps – just a desperate
    regular in need of pay and some way out
    of poverty and farms. Much better I not speak for you,
    since you left no words except your name.

October 1962

Ten years before I am born,
my father builds a wall,

slops gun-metal mortar
onto a row of bricks,

runs his trowel along each side
to make a neat mound of gloop

that's wet as his cap and his coat,
as cold as the airfield's tarmac.

Planes of a type he can't name
squat on the sodden horizon.

Men in slate-blue uniforms
tinker with metal cartridges

as big as themselves,
while my father presses brick

after brick into place,
letting the excess ooze

like jam between two halves
of sponge-cake, slapping it back

onto his board with a practised flick.
When the wall is done he packs

his flask and tools, shows
his pass at the gate, then waits

for a bus to town, taking in
the view from the ridge –

the flat expanse of the North
in its cape of mist, monochrome

like aerial photos of Cuba
he sees every night on the telly.

A country consumed by terrible heat.

You Explain to Me Your Plans for Surviving the End of Civilization as We Know It

The first thing is to forget the city.
When power fails, appliances will be
abandoned, their doors agape.

Fresh food's a waste of time. Tins
are easy to shift when faced with snipers
or an angry mob. Your mantra's

bandages, aspirin, matches, lint.
The journey out is covered –
you've plenty of petrol stored

and the car will make a shelter until
you find a house at the edge of woods,
a clear stream, a vantage from which

to pick out curls of smoke from conurbations
becoming ash. Your children will skin
jack-rabbits, no longer sentimental,

and you will spend long hours turning
the clockwork radio's dial, spinning
the chamber of your granddad's service revolver –

you tell me you're already oiling it every night.

How It Was

after Richard Pietraß

Black ink drying on a stamped permit.
>Home-made wine in the orchard at dusk.

Great cities falling dumb in winter.
>Table-talk in the halo of storm-lamps.

The necessary lies.
>The unavoidable truth.

A policeman thumbing documents
his sweat under nylon.
>The precious volume slipped into a pocket.

Blood in the mouth.
>Song in the head.

The wall.
>The man in work-boots scaling that wall.

The oath of allegiance
saluting the flag.
>An afternoon spent smoking by cool water.

The victory parade.
>Neighbours dancing drunk in the courtyard.

The smell of concrete and lignite-smoke.
>Someone playing guitar across the street.

A Journey

They picked me up on the corner and we drove,
pretended not to recognise each other,
smoked as we slid from the city's aura.
I leant forward to hear what talk there was

between men shy of their fictional names.
A petrol station. A carrier bag of lager
and crisps. We stamped our feet on the scraggy verge
as the owner turned his little sign to *CLOSED*.

The car plunged on through plains of darkness,
surfaced only in stray villages – their pubs
empty, blue light in the butchers' windows,
churches hewn from pure gravity.

At dawn, a frosted lane. We cut the radio,
fetched our gear from the cold boot and strode
to meet the old man as he rose to milk his cows –
cornered him, finally, in the floodlit yard.

Arcadia

Song of His Sooterkin Brother

For Angela France

Oh Ma – there is no charm or tune to make him
leave. Lizard-fingered he rides in the fold of your
sleeve, nuzzles and pecks at your wrist with the dry
comma of his nose. He has not spoken

or grown since we first slipped in your wake, two fish
flapping on a sheet. The burly midwife hoisted me,
gasping and shrill, while you were at his care,
groaning for love as you tongued his fur flat.

All our boyhood I scuffed the edges of fields,
haunted hawthorn lanes, whistled those airs that
comforted only him, as you rocked and cooed your
smaller treasure in his burrow of animal sleep.

Mother, I have been to sea, brought you
shells with an ocean in them, shocks of silk
they sell on Constantinople's quays – but only
my brother earns your looks and sighs. So tonight

I slip the latch. The moon-wet path is a stream
that runs to the coast and my canvas bag hangs raw
in my hand. I leave you both your land-locked love.
The ship is singing with the wind in her rigs and sails.

Murder Ballad

The forest like a bad old song, the hidden
doll, the torn cheek of a milking girl –
new lace in tatters, her bonnet in the midden.
The sergeant takes tea at every door and twirls
his 'tache. Another matron mourns her pearl,
as journeymen are made to swear on the Book.
The children watch the ponds, the mill-race, hurl
in rocks to dislodge a corpse, but nobody looks
to the lasses in lanes of eventide, where berries are shook

like the bloodied hem of a summer gown. The parson's cook
could swear she saw a shape shift by the brook.
And then it's the turn of the seamstress with the kiss-curl,
cut in half in a clearing and circled by rooks.
Autumn – gluey chestnut buds unfurl
and the north wind gutters green with the ash keys' whirl.
The trail gone cold in this silent land, though they didn't
think to ask that sweaty lad with the choirgirl
hands, whose father beats out all that's forbidden.

To the Harvesters of Ambergris

The ocean's darkness rings thickest in the bell
of the whale's stomach, a note swelled
      and sluiced as the creature feeds on time,
      winnows echoes of the drowned from brine

that coalesce as nodules in the vault of its back.
When the ocean shakes, these corms of black
      softness are loosened like spores into fog,
      bob up in the hard waves that tug

insistent at the shores and spumy headlands.
You coast-folk find that shit-smelling contraband –
      rabbit-sized, tarry to the touch like the hull
      of a flat-bottomed skiff. Secret. Full.

Then the wind comes on, these gifts are bleached
with grit and sun. Now scavenge the beach
      for that denser resin. Scrape
      it for your fearful incense, steeped

in oils. Mix it with cloves and camphor
to infuse earthenware amphoras,
      before the thin-lipped customs men come
      to cart the stash away. Some

say it goes to prick the god-love
in ravaged priests, some say to move
      the melancholy sea-widows
      finally to tears. But you know

what scent, or rhythm or song prevails
in seams, in skin, under fingernails.

The End of a Film with Jimmy Stewart

Jimmy in his disgruntled hat and holiday loafers,
heaving valises into the trunk of his car.
In this life he has kids, a staid, ironic wife,
and has not fallen for the flinty blonde,
was never broken by villains in monochrome.

His daughter may be sixteen in a lemon sweater,
pining for that unsuitable boy, but even he
may turn out to be okay after all. This summer
the family learned a lot about each other,
and this time nobody even had to die.

Jimmy shuts up the rented clapboard beach-house
that will seem a little haunted when they are gone.
Final heat leeches from the season
the way an itch at last goes out of a scar.
The ocean folds its hands across the bay

as Jimmy steers for a milky horizon,
forgetting the locals just as he waves them goodbye.

Driving Back to Lincolnshire for a Funeral

Geese made their arrow in the sky,
wavered like ink in a glass of drinking-water,
black as a glob of liquorice on the tongue.
I dipped beneath them, my knackered engine's song
percussed along the splashy tarmac, all splutter
and choke. I only seemed to say goodbye

when I returned. The flatland boiled the sun
in roiling mist, a rhythm of funeral parades
swung slow in lonesome trees, and the radio said
whatever it wanted, played its jaunty undead
tunes of yesteryear, while jiving shades
in airforce blue imported American fun

to clapped-out dance-halls in corrugated hangars.
Lost world of tiny monochrome snaps – hair-do-ed
girls, then wives in pinnies or pillbox hats,
gardens strung with plenty by blokes in caps,
Formica and snazzy cuts announcing the new.
Time has no taste, death no manners –

like cheeky spivs, they sidle up and whisper,
Now! Then now is past. The plan, such as
it was, has gone awry as all must go,
leaving the sundown to say *We told you so*,
the dusk to pile up its unforgiving ash.
No escape, not even by a whisker,

much less by one of these country miles. The village
rounded into view, its straggle of Forties
council houses, then the des-res homes
packed tight against that winter's useless moan
and ache, roads slick-sliding with mud from lorries,
loaded up with mucky beets or silage

for cattle, dreaming in their barn-sweet drowse,
or sheep that picked like ghosts at frozen stalks
in vanishing fields. That ice was in my bones
as well, their clack and scrape, the fear-drummed drone
of blood in my ears when I couldn't sleep, the mawk-
ish chiding of my past in sharp-toothed hours.

I stepped into the rain-whipped dark and hollered –
Just give me some years when no-one at all will die!
But the earth was wrestling in December's arms
and could not hear, its long nights steeped in harm
and half-remembered hope. I steered for the lights
of the house and slunk for home. The darkness followed.

Paysage marin

If we saved this blue to send the women
swatches of our keening night, unhurried
stars and smokes all playing chicken
with the dark, this glare could not be carried
save in sinews, its brazen logic buried
fathoms deep in us. The hours occur
like happy thoughts. So strange and sudden married,
we who taste this salt and think it queer
but kind. My love, be still. You must not jink or jeer

at this soft talk. Whatever is from you I smear
across my torso (yours thickly gleamed in fur)
and think upon how love is fleshly varied.
There is no wage of sin we could incur.
The tower of wants and needs so many-storied,
only busy gods could build it. We've wearied,
yes, but let your self lie here and listen!
The sea now whispers of the souls it's ferried.
Let me pull you straight like table linen.

Ode to Achilles

Praised be Achilles, as he serves beer in frosted tumblers.
    Light-haired, he could be American, save for that fluid
    heat in his bones. Should we suppose he'll shake it out
    tonight in narrow rooms, while tourists close their sweaty
    eyes, cicadas saw the last of their music?

Proud Achilles knows the names of broom and lentisk,
    reaches to cup the pink and white of oleander
    in arid lanes. These afternoons, we come to praise him,
    strong Achilles, who shaves his chest-hair, as we cannot
    help but notice when he leans to fill our glasses.

How easy we would feel to have Achilles hold
    the tiller of the brittle caïque that's chartered to set us
    ashore. If we asked, he might well say that girls
    are plentiful as citrus, that he must only reach
    a hand, sensing cold fruit shudder for his touch.

Oh, praise again Achilles, even as he turns away,
    showing the sun the place he might be wounded.

In Hangzhou

Wearing my coat back-to-front
I rode my electric moped to work –
selling liquor from jars of ginseng
and reptile. Across the street, an old man
was drying tea for the tourists, thick
green palms caressing hot copper.
By the West Lake I watched gardeners
harvesting persimmon fruit like globes
of fire, plucked from silken mist.
Beneath the water, the white snake-demon
writhed, banished for daring
to love a human man. At weekends,
I'd climb to the temples to glow in the laughter
of fat-bellied Buddha, or watch the golden
thin-faced Buddha pouring the ocean
from his cup. Sometimes I prayed
for long life, mostly for the birth
of a son. Later I sauntered
down Slow Life Street, burnt
sugar and sesame stuck to my teeth,
finding suddenness at every corner.
I thought of Nixon's hand-made limo,
polished black and chrome on a sheet
of creamy marble. And then I knew
I'd never lived in this city at all.

Exodus

Gay Pride Festival, Clapham Common, 1996

I remember, chiefly, that shocking light,
how we squinted up from the earth,
bleached by the very summer that floored us –

how through that light emerged those thin-armed
boys from my class, proclaiming themselves
the heralds of memory, even that one

I'd hit for calling me queer. Now
our lustrous presence was all the proof
required. We sucked at cans of Red Stripe,

lounged in glare like exiles thrown
on a luminous shore, scuffing at it,
heel by heel, until the dust

threw up another move. Come
to think, we already had the people
we needed – hawkers of ironic

T-shirts and merchants of the old
religion, saving us all in brand new
drag. But then someone was grabbing

the mic. A thousand balloons cut loose
from their net, a pulsing vermilion
arc, while men made little huddles

of grief in twos and threes, their faces
tight with fat and beautiful tears.
I stalked to the edge of the crowd, chippy

as some lad who just missed out
on the war. A whole new country was set
before me, refusing to be ignored.

Substance

Candy

Trouser that change from the milkman, clammy coppers
and silver queens your dad chucks on his desk –
they'll not be missed. We're out of the yard, brisk
in the after home-time hush. Proper
spies, agents of the sugar rush.

Our contact's Mr Moody, who sells the news
and every kind of chew, bonbon or fizz.
He grimaces like a hard-faced fence, too shrewd
to fool himself our cash is kosher. Humbugs,
kola kubes, bullseyes, pear drops, aniseed twists.

We slope behind the reccy's huts and test
our cracking teeth. Citric acid burns
the gums, blisters prick on the scarlet tips
of tongues. Gut-rot. Jaw-ache. Head-throb. Bliss.

1/8

Shifty blokes ease their beat-up Jags
into the sleep of these suburbs, slow where neon
yellows the pitted paths by take-aways.
Daft lads play with plastic lighters, wait

to swap their tight-rolled tenners for an eighth –
foil-wrapped orient charm they snug away
in a hot hip-pocket, putting on
their most innocent slouch. Splitting fags

in upstairs rooms, they crumble resin, drag
at the charring cone that showers a million
particles of silence. There's nothing to say
on these nights before life begins – so they bathe

in the skylight's darkness, fogged by their famished
dreams, let pin-holes burn in their plans to vanish.

Gran Reserva

The table talk goes on. I turn the shining
demi-globe, stretch my fun-house reflection
in its gloss. The scent of bitter grapeskin
spills in fuzzy air, conjures something

farmyard, silage even – fermented rot
of that late summer, six years gone. The knot
of sex that bound us working loose in sober
mornings, the glass I drank when it was over,

sitting in my coat at the kitchen table. You'd say
I'm only drowning troubles, but a connoisseur
of consolation savours sorrow, honer
of his melancholy metier.

For me, a man must love his art, its cost –
choose his poison, drain it to the last.

Halfzware Shag

You'd learned to roll one-handed, in a gale at a sodden
bus-stop, then fed me the seed of my own addiction
in stray, bitter strands that stuck to lips
and tongue, the after-burn of your saliva
billowing from my mouth, ghost of a kiss
suggested but withheld. Bleary survivors
of nights in cellar bars, we squatted smoking
in your bedsit, clothed in each other's fumes –
noxious, turning daylight to fog in that room's
hot enclosure. Sometimes you'd pass the tin
and let me try my hand. A different thrill –
your lungs awash with my charred DNA,
a sense that those who serve also betray,
the knowledge that acts of love can slowly kill.

Powder

I saw you slide home, sour from a stranger's bed,
as morning clattered in over Swansea Bay.
Your words were all used up, the drug had fizzed
to nothing. So you bored a tunnel into day,
your exhaustion cut with the ash of last night's beats.

In time, you came to hate the fleshless daylight,
like the hero hexed by his dance with the faerie crowd,
who returns to their camp-fire night after blazing night
until their potions take on the tang of defeat.

The crystals scorched your throat and made you loud,
you talked us half to death with your big plans.
Out on the floor you'd swoon into someone's hands
and make your exit, blowing diva kisses –
to become, at last, the man who nobody misses.

Boats

Those white ones and the ones the colour of yellow earth,
or black as damp ashes, blue like the Holy Virgin's mantle;

tacked together from blistered timbers, or strung with blades
    of oak,
so the ocean plays them like shivering harps –
otherwise, wedges of bolted steel which open the waves;

the boats which carry jugs of perfumed wine,
sweet chunks of marble, batteries and plastic shoes,
censored tracts, and so many pots
whose mouths are stopped with wax or clay,
vouched with seals of Mycenaean merchants,
others with dubious certificates of provenance;

also, the harried bodies of chancers and exiles
– Africans, Syrians, Persians –
pressed in greasy engine rooms,
or reading their prospects from a billow of sail,
or lulled by the muscular creak of oars.

I wish them all safe harbours.

From Here

A Family Romance

Say there's this boy
at the head of a valley
leaning on handle-bars,
watching a house below
whose gable end is torn,
the seam of stones
having worked apart.
Say the landlord refuses to fix it,
offers only a straining sail of blue
tarpaulin to cover the gash,
for the reason he's waiting on winter
to freeze out his tardy renters.
They are, let's suppose,
four sisters in kohl and jumble sale dresses
sowing paperbacks, gossip mags,
sleeveless vinyl discs of jazz
in their mesmerising wake;
then probably also a pack of various hounds
lurching from room to room, running
the cottage's native vermin
to ground. There'll be a mother, of course,
who surveys the teetering mounds of dirty dishes
amused, a JPS clamped in her lips;
and doubtless also a father who keeps
to a silent nook, sketches his latest
scheme to capture the dark.
Finally, there must be a brooding son,
a bitter artist coughing on some complaint.
But here's the boy with the bike again,
head ducked under the wind, cycling down

to tap at their rattling door,
to play his part as – of course! –
the lad from the farm, hair matted
with sweat, face shining with expectation.
Eventually, we guess, he'll be led
through the din of these alien folk
to a draughty upstairs room,
and then we'll know how this story really begins.

From Here

At the back of the house, traffic noise teases leylandii.
Pigeons alight in apple trees, grapple unsteady
branches and dislodge the last of this year's fruit.
Tough of hide, sharp of juice, the toppermost

drop like fuseless bombs on a mulch of lawn
to startle cats as they weave through fencing, feverfew.
And I have an itch in my heart to be out of here,
bootsoles licking the rainsheen on bitumen, to plot

my course around a ring road and catch the spur
of a lane that gestures weakly to hills, the sea
beyond. At the proper distance I might observe
this place that mugs it up as fate, though some

would call it a coward's choice. From there, perhaps,
I'd know what this means – to settle, to be sited, to dwell.
A neighbour's boiler groans and spits, the uncleared
guttering splutters rounds of shot on concrete paths,

while in the garden three plastic chairs,
arranged to seat a council of summer's ghosts,
fill up with lichen pools of shivering stuff.
Streetlights morse on-off as evening nears.

On Assembling and Disassembling
a Greenhouse

We bought it second-hand,
　in pieces –

spent hours twirling
　　　aluminium struts
and spars
　　　perplexed, like useless
majorettes.
　　　Then an arc of ribs
　rose up,
a mail of
sun-gorged panes.
It was, we saw, the last
of its kind, adrift among vines,
its hide tattooed by cobweb, snail-spit.
It lost its sight by degrees to knot-weed, dust,
flies bobbed in its vacant head and brambles pressed
their shoots between its scales. Now we,
who are not so inclined to settle
in this greening place,
have filleted
heat and
　　　glass
　　　　　from its bones.
　　　The carcass,
　　　　　skinless,
a museum exhibit,
　　　shivers,
　　　　　whistles
　　　　　　　on cleared ground.

See England by Train

See the hauliers' yards and pyres of scrap,
        the pallets stacked, bone-blonde,
in scraggy pasture. Witness the doubtful
        pomp of orange plastic netting,
pearls of polystyrene tussled in briar.

Note how rural stations imply
        unpeopled streets, clothes-lines sagging
with knickers, goosed by recidivist
        breezes. Then abandon these for neat
openings of playing field, golf course,

as thin sun greases the hollows.
        Behold this land, a scrim of dun,
and grey and verdigris, pinned inexpertly
        to a sad sky by rows of pylons.
And England's sons cowering

beneath the ancient shrug of iron bridges
        or slack by drums of blue-ish cable.
Its daughters, also, straddling abandoned
        lengths of concrete pipe, their laughter
blown back upon them like smoke
        in muzzy rain.

News from Home

Nobody misses you. They never will
      while there's silence to hear the kettle tick
as it cools, the traffic's susurration
      through double-glazing. Your daughter pulls
the front door gently into its frame
      behind her, surveys the vista of evening,
dry-eyed and charged with purpose. And your now
      ex-wife subsides in a tub of lilac
and steam, hums to herself and imagines
      those days to come now emptied of you,
how she'll fill them. The crockery's snug in the dark,
      the doors unslammed, a coat of paint
has soothed that stain on the wall. A guest
      would think this dent in the sofa
could have been made by any arse.

To *The Gloucestershire Echo*

A cut-price oracle, succour to the outraged –
      its name is hawked in our streets by grizzled acolytes,
its rollable self stuffed through our letterboxes
      by breathless mercuries in anoraks,

or rammed into jacket pockets by scoundrels leaving
      public houses. So malleable, so unburdened by vanity,
it never complains of creases, crumbs or unattributed stains,
      never protests to be left on buses,

flicked through by cheapskates who find it under their seats.
      No fool for subtleties,
it spins its Manichean visions
      and leave us in thrall to the neatest of worlds,

where busy mums and doting granddads
      are pitted against proprietors of crack-houses
and aldermen who do not answers letters.
      And though no great stylist

(such are its democratic convictions)
      it blesses us daily with poetry
penned by its in-house surrealist collective:
      'False leg raises charity cash' – 'Lover stole dog's ashes.'

Boon of the altruistic, a booster of cakes stalls
      and memorial benches – for these civic virtues
we forgive its occasional prurience, its po-faced dispatches
      on raided brothels and kinky schoolmasters

lecturing the Lower Sixth on bondage.
  A literary mayfly, transience is its element –
who else expresses such conviction
  with oblivion at their back?

Domestic Gods

We salvaged wood from unbuilt bookshelves,
untangled Christmas lights, searched for gaffer tape.
Squeezing the last of the out-of-date SuperGlue,
we lit a ring of power-cut candles.

We tacked up photos of fleshy starlets,
sprinkled ash of *billet doux*,
arranged a zigzag of plastic pearls
around an egg-timer shaped like a chicken

and three holographic Tarot postcards
(The Tower, The Warrior, The Picker of Pockets);
but, standing back, you were still disappointed
with our make-shift shrine to domestic gods.

So we danced a syncretic hokey-cokey,
kicked up a mystic cha-cha-cha,
you oiled and burned a lock of my hair,
said your secret backwards prayer.

Shed

The smell of sack-cloth, hot in the earth of years.
How it shifted beneath us, sprayed motes into air,
fibres that stippled muted sun. And how
my hand felt, as it steadied itself on a bench of wood

so buffed and bronzed it might have been a mammoth's
knotty hide. Outside, the daylight was broad,
but we preferred the narrow between the lumber,
jars your dad had filled with nails and grease.

We heard the roof-felt slowly melt, a slither
of pitch and grit, while smoothness extended under
our palms and we followed that curve from lowest rib
to cusp of hip, slid to the top of the thigh.

than you expected

The beginning easier
The answer more simple
The summer hotter
The sex rougher

The flat more expensive
The walls damper
The bedstead more creaky
The neighbours less friendly

His possessions fewer
His family more distant
His plans vaguer
The money scarcer

Your job harder
Your boss more a bastard
The bus less reliable
Your heart more tired

His silences darker
His absences longer
The storm more frightening
The moon less a comfort

His mood more brittle
His jokes nastier
The news less shocking
The police much kinder

The whole thing over sooner

For Hanna on Her 50ᵗʰ Birthday

Waking, you may find this summer morning drear
on the valley – tossed trees explaining the wind, deer
couchant in the couch-grass. The garden door

invites first grey, then – look! – a tug of blue, all dire
prediction overthrown as the lawn steams itself drier.
The ones you love pad the house, drawn

from private sleep, yet never supposing you a dreamer.
This homely rhythm glows in you like a warm dram,
leaves you vibrating, a struck drum.

About the Ocean

The ocean imagines its tides are embraces,
whose rush and pull recall how our cells
once jittered and flowed in one matter.

As if salt on the tongue were nostalgia,
or siren calls would spook the plumbing;
those pools of memory abandoned in fields.

But mostly, we stare dumb at the ocean,
as we might watch cows or trees,
or notice it less than the light that moves

through the house in the length of a day.

House of the Artist

We worked so hard to get things as he left them –
  splashed cold tea on rugs, smeared our hands
    in oils before we opened cupboards, lovingly
      soiled their contents. One half-day, we smoked
        ten packs of his unfashionable brand, lips slick
          in those distinctive shades of gloss
            his last three muses wore. Their whimpers
        of frustration, sighs and after door-slam
      silences were looped on CD
  in upstairs rooms. Still he remained immensely
    gone. We tried the ouija, thumped away
      at his favourite songs on every untuned piano
        in the place, gave chorus to his trademark
          hacking cough. The three-bar fire still glowed,
        but could not raise a whiff of his damp-trousered
    calves. Opening day saw us desperate,
  the car park full of dignitaries and press.
I ran to an unfinished canvas, held
  a brush a hair's breadth from its surface,
    kept the pose. And there he was.

Author Photograph

The poet is writing at a kitchen table,
leaving aside the fiscal implications. Leadership
is ultimately about knowing when to say yes.

The poet is dinkering with a pipe,
not realising the potential of big data.
Maybe, but again maybe not.

The poet is on a hillside,
showing that the point is not to demonise,
but to understand. Language should not be a barrier.

The poet has big hair and a powerful gaze.
Ripped bodies are taking centre stage this year.
Visions. Hot-button issues. Feeling pretty chillaxed.

Notes and Acknowledgements

'Song of his Sooterkin Brother' refers to the folklore of the sooterkin that I first encountered in Angela France's poem 'Living with the Sooterkin' from her collection *Hide* (Nine Arches Press, 2013).

The quotation from Didier Fassin and Richard Reitman in 'The Psychiatrist Addresses His Patient, a Soldier' is from their book *The Empire of Trauma: An Inquiry into the Condition of Victimhood*, translated by Rachel Gomme (Princeton University Press, 2009).

Thanks are due to the editors of the following anthologies, journals and websites for publishing some of these poems or earlier versions of them: *Lunar Poetry, Amaryllis, Nothing Recognisable as Human: Poems from the Poetry Space Competition 2013* (Poetryspace), *The Great British Bard Off, South Bank Poetry, The Poetry Shed, Under the Radar, Sentinel Literary Quarterly, The Cannon's Mouth, New Walk, Kumquat, Other Countries: Contemporary Poets Rewiring History* (ed. by Claire Trévien and Gareth Prior), Wells Festival of Literature Poetry Competition, The Ver Prize 2014, Battered Moons Poetry Competition 2013, *Cast: The Poetry Business Book of New Contemporary Poets* (Smith|Doorstop), *The Museum of Light* (Yew Tree Press), *The Interpreter's House, South, Antiphon, Magma, Live Canon Anthology 2012*. Some of these poems also appeared in my pamphlet, *Gaud* (Flarestack Poets). I remain grateful to Jacqui Rowe and Meredith Andrea of Flarestack Poets for their wonderful support. Thanks also to Helen Dewbery for the author photograph.

Several of these poems were written during a residency in Greece sponsored by the Michael Marks Charitable Trust. I would like to thank the Trust for its generosity and the staff of the Harvard Centre for Hellenic Studies for their hospitality. My thanks, also, to Andrew Forster for being such a good-humoured travelling companion.

I would like to express my gratitude to the people who have read and commented on some of these poems over the last five years: David Briggs, Rachael Boast, Chaucer Cameron, Angela France, Sharon Larkin, Philip Rush, Anna Saunders and Avril Staple. I am particularly indebted to my poetry advisor, Jennie Farley, for her support and encouragement. Finally, my thanks go to Jane Commane of Nine Arches Press for brilliant editing and her faith in this collection.